ADAM L.S.

The Fellowship

First published by Raguel Studios 2024

First edition

Illustration by Dean Snider
Editing by Karen Keeline

This book was professionally typeset on Reedsy.
Find out more at reedsy.com

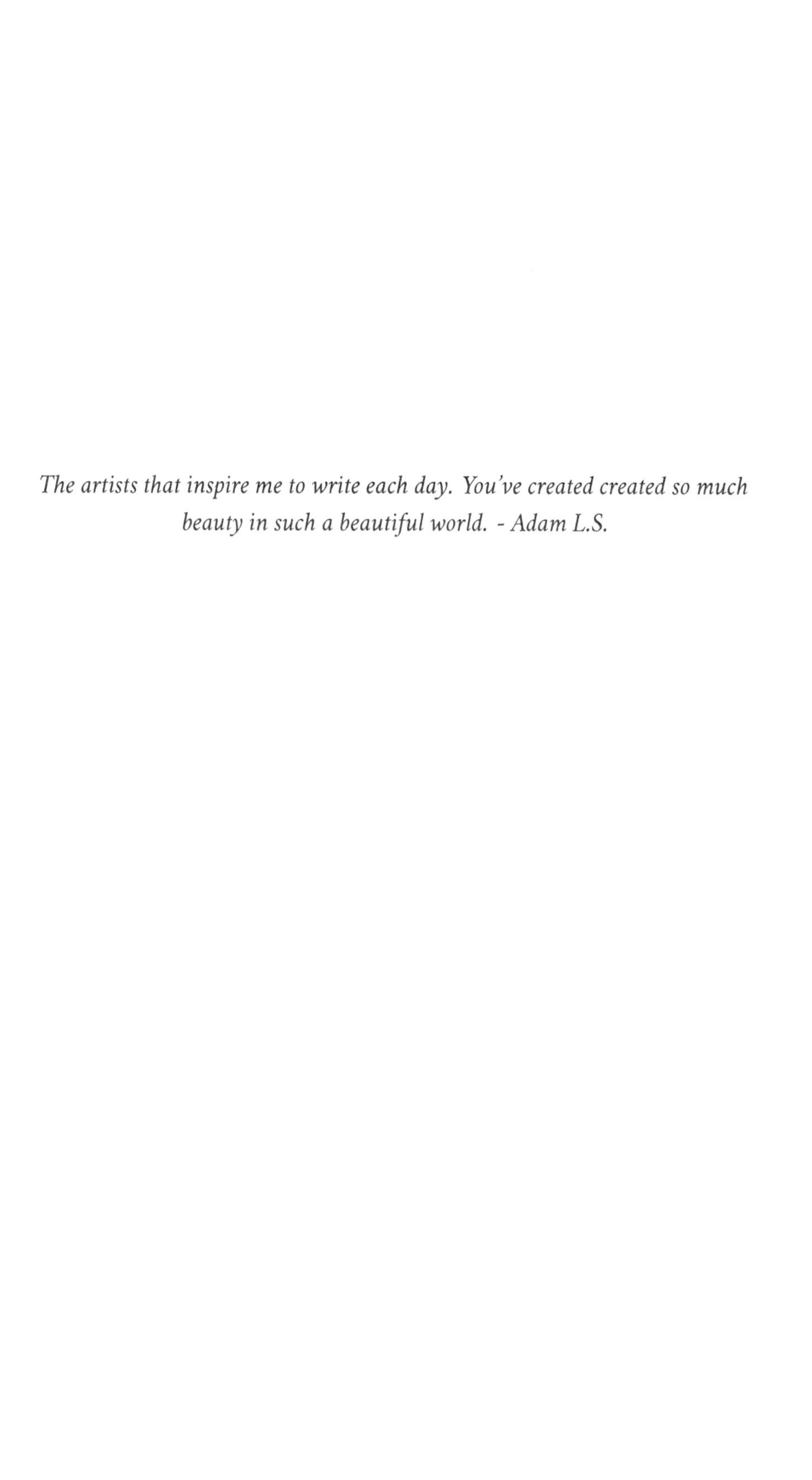

The artists that inspire me to write each day. You've created created so much beauty in such a beautiful world. - Adam L.S.

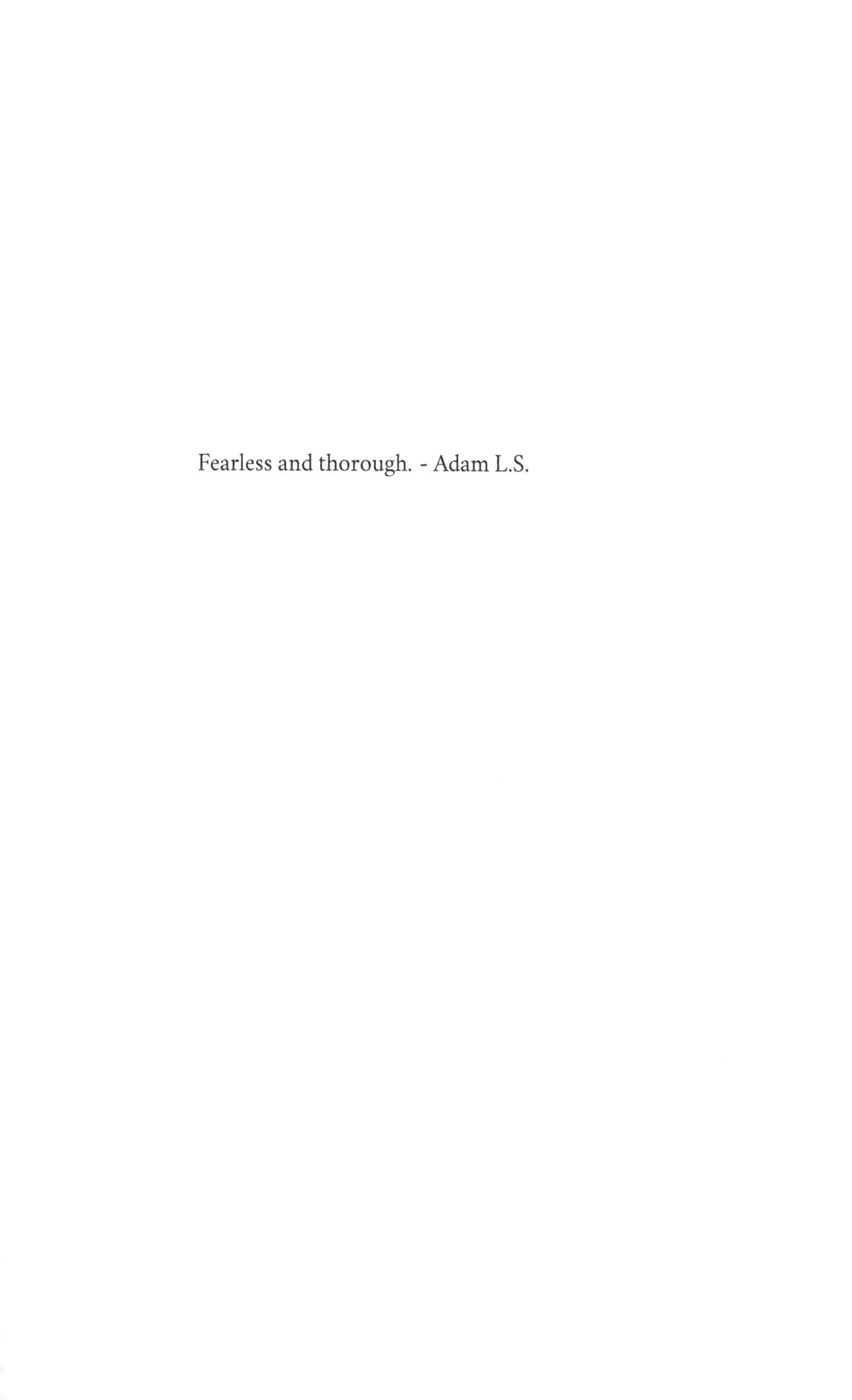

Fearless and thorough. - Adam L.S.

Contents

Acknowledgments v
Example 1
Bonds 2
Recover 3
Pieces 4
Made It 5
Pyramid 6
Instrumental 7
In A Book 8
They 9
A Marker 10
Speak Up 11
Me 12
One Book 13
Common Welfare 14
Present 15
Addicts 16
Strength In Numbers 17
A Parent 18
Come With Me 19
Volumes 20
Keep Going 21
We 22
Say What 23
Follow It 24
Superman 25

Amazing 26
The Memo 27
Truly 28
New New 29
Books Written 30
Another Form 31
Only 32
Detection 33
Alien 34
Back Then 35
Oops 36
That Road 37
Devoured 38
Crazy Town 39
Dead End 40
Reservation 41
The Pit 42
Cocoon 43
Forgotten 44
Call 45
Realization 46
Another Chance 47
Abstinence 48
All Of This 49
New Here 50
Improving 51
Lead 52
This Program 53
Capable 54
Looking Glass 55
Finale 56
Realization 57
Full Stop 58

The Fellowship 59
Ready Up 60
The Room Where It Happens 61
Hope 62
Weapon 63
It's Time 64
Go 65
I Am 66
I'll Pass 67
It Works 68
Enough Is Enough 69
Probably Both 70
Addiction 71
That Road 72
Quitter 73
That's It 74
Searching 75
No More 76
Unlock 77
Admit 78
The Admission 79
All Has Been Revealed 80
My Part 81
Remove 82
Moving Forward 83
Seven Layers 84
Truly 85
Amends 86
Just Do It 87
It's Possible 88
Best Of The Best 89
Almost There 90
Unresolved 91

Wrong 92
Searching 93
Difficulties 94
Counter Clockwise 95
Examine 96
Higher Power 97
Your Will 98
Clock Struck 99
More Meaning 100
Also by Adam L.S. 101

Acknowledgments

To my friends and family, y'all have been there for me through so much. You are my Fellowship. - Adam L.S.

Example

Simplicity…
  How is that the key?

Let the Fellowship show you.

Adam L.S.

Bonds

It's easily found,
  its easily understood...

The relationships present,
  the relationships formed...

Between these walls,
  in these seats.

Adam L.S.

Recover

The recovering...

Defined.
  Seen.
  Understood.

A membership to this society is free.

Adam L.S.

Pieces

I wanted to do the right thing,
  when I was in my right mind.

I was not fully whole,
  before I sought to be of service,
  and to live for God's will.

Adam L.S.

Made It

Climbing…
  Rising…
  Grasping…

For freedom.
  Got it!

Adam L.S.

Pyramid

At the point of no return,
  or complete freedom.

Every turn,
  every side...

There they stood.

Adam L.S.

Instrumental

It's open,
  it's free,
  it's just down the street...

Our meetings,
  our groups,
  our recovery.

Adam L.S.

In A Book

We carried it,
  we breathed it,
  we experienced it.

With the message of hope…
  We stayed clean.

Adam L.S.

They

I had come unraveled,
  the threads so strong,
  it would be a challenge gathering them all.

It would work,
  they have experience.

Adam L.S.

A Marker

I have a lot of life left to live,
   not on my terms tho,
   I have to recover.

The means are there,
   growing thru the pains of it all,
   coming of age, doing His will.

Adam L.S.

Speak Up

My ability,
  to change….

My voice,
  to be used…

I spoke to many.

Adam L.S.

Me

The aim…
  The goal…

The richness…
  the recovery…

This is what I look like now.

Adam L.S.

One Book

I had a vision,
  of living in the world…

There's hope.

Adam L.S.

Common Welfare

So many walks…
  Faith, philosophy…

Each unfolding the world…
  These walks of life…

These ideals of unity.

Adam L.S.

Present

This is my true spirit…

I ran from it before.
  I had to find my voice.
  I had to find my foundation.

We are uniquely equal.

Adam L.S.

Addicts

I walked thru the doors,
   I heard the message.

They said you are welcome here,
   they showed me a new way to live.

Together we…
   Grow
   Change
   Recover

Adam L.S.

Strength In Numbers

The topic today is…
  Personal experiences.

I have a few of those… So do they.

Adam L.S.

A Parent

It was apparent,
  the boy needed direction.

It was apparent,
  the man found his purpose.

Adam L.S.

Come With Me

Complete effort,
  Complete structure,
  Complete contribution.

Completely assembled.
  Collective conscience.

Adam L.S.

Volumes

Every single…
  Story,
  idea,
  cup,
  laugh,
  tear,
  heartbeat.

Adam L.S.

Keep Going

Every addict,
  seeking recovery,
  knows about the pain,
  that they caused.

It's time,
  to share this desire,
  for recovery,
  with gratitude.

Keep going!

Adam L.S.

We

We change,
  the nature of the addict,
  the old lie.

We are,
  the recovered,
  the available.

Remember this.

Adam L.S.

Say What

This book has been shared,
this experience,
this proven plan,
this program,
this was to a new life…

Is beautiful.

Adam L.S.

Follow It

Guided down the same path,
  I am grateful for these directions.

It leads to recovery,
  I am grateful for this foundation.

Adam L.S.

Superman

The solution…

Is the hope I found.

Adam L.S.

Amazing

Our potential,
  our spirit,
  our solution…

Our recovery!
  Is amazing.

Adam L.S.

The Memo

God,
  your work,
  your will…

Not ours.

Adam L.S.

Truly

The bond of selflessness.
  Truly.

I'm done with the horrors of addiction.
  Truly.

A sense of your purpose.
  Truly.

Adam L.S.

New New

I'm new.

This is new.
  That's new.

I remained clean.

Adam L.S.

Books Written

This book outlines the nature of our recovery.
Give yourself a bit of a break.

Adam L.S.

Another Form

Who is…
  That is a great question.

Who lived…
  To use and used to live.

We were in it's grip…
  It progressed.

Jails, institutions and death.

Adam L.S.

Only

Mind altering,
  mood changing substance.

We knew it was there.
  We know we can stop.

In desperation, found a new way to live.

Adam L.S.

Detection

I stopped for a while,
  I thought of it less and less.

I suffered,
  I got more and more.

I was antisocial,
  I found life difficult.

Adam L.S.

Alien

Isolated,
  hostile,
  resentful,
  self centered,
  self seeking.

I did not know how to be part of,
  part of the outside world.

Adam L.S.

Back Then

Dangerous,
  was the story of my life.

I used to survive,
  this was the only way I knew.

Adam L.S.

Oops

I said…
  I can handle it.
  I couldn't.

This idea…
  This vision of hope,
  this jail cell.

My path…
  My moral code,
  my ego.

So many misconceptions.

Adam L.S.

That Road

Driven deeper into desperation.
  I lied, stole, cheated.
  Regardless of the cost.
  Failure and fear invaded.

Adam L.S.

Devoured

I could not deal with life,
I had to have it to cope.
I dreamed of a magic formula.
I justified it all.
I was consumed by fear and self pity.
I displayed a pattern of selective thinking.

Adam L.S.

Crazy Town

I kept going crazy,
  my life was a nightmare.

I avoided reality,
  my ability to love was affected.

I was an animal,
  my spirit was broken.

I exhibited an extreme state of mind,
  my behavior made me incapable of finding an answer.

Adam L.S.

Dead End

I imagined the end,
   being near.

I was feeble,
   being worthless.

I was trapped in the illusion,
   "just one more time."

Adam L.S.

Reservation

I thought I had it under control,
  even though I was on my knees.

I was unwilling to admit,
  I was lost.

Adam L.S.

The Pit

My enabler,
  was my point of view.

My addiction,
  was my downfall.

I had no concern for my well being,
  or the well being of others.

Adam L.S.

Cocoon

So strange,
  my habits,
  my mannerisms.

Social graces were non existent.

Adam L.S.

Forgotten

I forgot what it was like to feel,
  I forgot what it was like to be alive.

Adam L.S.

Call

Don't die from this,
  don't go to prison,
  don't keep going back to institutions,
  don't cave to demoralization.

I don't want to give into this disease anymore.
  I picked up the phone.

Adam L.S.

Realization

I was a slave,
I was in a prisoner of my own mind.

It was progressive,
It could have been fatal.

Adam L.S.

Another Chance

I began by stopping,
   not caring when it began,
   or how,
   never being cured,
   in me always…

I still recovered.

Adam L.S.

Abstinence

One requirement for membership,
just stop.

Be open minded,
give yourself a break.

Adam L.S.

All Of This

I replaced those old ideas with new ones,
  I allowed the program to work miracles in my life,
  I became a different person,
  I kept coming back.

Adam L.S.

New Here

They said I was the most important person in the room,
  that felt so odd,
  however it was so sweet.

I believed I was the least important person alive,
  so it helped.

Adam L.S.

Improving

There was a miracle happening,
   in my life, in theirs.

I know I'm a different person today.

Adam L.S.

Lead

Living it,
  gave me so much.

A relationship,
  with Him and others.

It helped,
  so now I am helpful.

Adam L.S.

This Program

I could not…
  Manage.
  Live.
  Enjoy.

I could…
  Ask.
  Grow.
  Serve.

Adam L.S.

Capable

I had to do this,
  at all costs.

I am now capable of facing life.

Adam L.S.

Looking Glass

I see it now,
   I was committed to fear.

It was so cunning,
   it is baffling.

Now, I seek you.

Adam L.S.

Finale

I thought I was doing what was necessary,
  when I'd sit there using,
  it was about surviving.

I thought it was OK,
  they'd cry,
  it wasn't OK.

I wasn't OK then,
  I am now,
  and so are they.

Adam L.S.

Realization

Handle it!
  Face life!
  Get up!
  Have fun!
  Smile!

More often.

Adam L.S.

Full Stop

They tried to help,
  they never lost hope,
  that'd I'd stop.

Success.

Adam L.S.

The Fellowship

Lost, to feeling like a failure,
this had become the only path I walked,

Lost, my self esteem was non existent,
the path had become so rugged.

Lost, each step was painful,
desperation, isolation, denial.

Found, I encountered others,
on another path, it went uphill.

They referred to themselves as the Fellowship.

Adam L.S.

Ready Up

Feeling like a complete failure,
change was needed.

These self destructive patterns could not continue,
degrading myself in my own eyes.

I was finally ready.

The Room Where It Happens

I sat there…
   One meeting…
   Two meetings…
   Several meetings…

I began to feel…

People cared!

Adam L.S.

Hope

No matter my past thoughts and actions,
  my fellow addicts said…

We recover,
  no matter what,
  you are not alone.

They gave me hope.

Adam L.S.

Weapon

I had to stop blaming…
  I had to face my problems and feelings.

I discovered the ultimate weapon.
  People like me.

Adam L.S.

It's Time

It's time,
  for a change of playmates, playgrounds and playthings.

It's time,
  to manage now,
  in these rooms,
  with these people,
  with this foundation.

Adam LS

Go

New opportunities.
  New sense of self worth.
  New level of self respect.
  New freedom.

Set it off.

Adam L.S.

I Am

It works,
  I am ready,
  recovery is possible,
  I am turning it over to Him,
  I am awake and I am on a spiritual journey.

Adam L.S.

I'll Pass

A huge order,
   A huge attitude.

This disease had a huge appetite.

Adam L.S.

It Works

Being completely realistic…
 The value in living comes from helping others.

Adam L.S.

Enough Is Enough

A thousand nights wasn't enough,
  when I believed I wasn't enough.

I was confused.
  I am.

Adam L.S.

Probably Both

Coincidences or miracles?
  Probably both.

Acceptance or trust?
  Probably both.

Higher Power or strength?
  Probably both.

Adam L.S.

Addiction

It changed me…

I was at odds with myself.
  I was isolating.
  I was deceitful.
  I was spiritually bankrupt.

I thought of oblivion.

Adam L.S.

That Road

I could not continue,
  if I did I could not live.

Adam LS.

Quitter

Two choices…

Suffer withdrawal or take more.
I withdrew.

Adam L.S.

That's It

All I had to do…

Was try.
  Say guide me.
  Say show me.

Adam L.S.

Searching

Searching.
  Fearless.

With this inventory I discovered something amazing…

I discovered who I really am.
  I discovered how to rid myself of the burdens and traps.

Adam L.S.

No More

Each step was crucial…

That fear was just a lack of faith.
  I found a loving God I could turn to.
  I no longer needed to be afraid.

Adam L.S.

Unlock

I was an expert,
   at self deception.

I am expert,
   at overcoming obstacles.

I will be an expert,
   at loving you and our family.

Adam L.S.

Admit

I admitted to…
  God.
  Myself.
  Others.

The exact nature of it.
  I was set free.
  I lived clean.
  I am in the present.
  I found the key to freedom.

Adam L.S.

The Admission

More about patterns,
  more about behaviors,
  more about actions.

It would need to come from my lips.

Adam L.S.

All Has Been Revealed

Would you reject me if you knew?
  I was unsure, uncomfortable, unrealistic.

I know now that you understand me.
  What I did and why I did it.

Adam L.S.

My Part

I could not procrastinate.
  I could not keep fooling them or myself.

I could be exact.
  I could tell the truth.

Adam L.S.

Remove

Remove them…

Each and every defect.
  I will work hard.
  I will let them all go.

Adam L.S.

Moving Forward

I embraced what I knew.
In fear of stepping into the unknown.

Adam L.S.

Seven Layers

Remove my shortcomings…

They cause so much pain and suffering.

Adam L.S.

Truly

Relieve me of those useless parts,
I'll be completely honest going forward.

I know...
There will always be room for growth.
It will be intense.
I will be well.

Adam L.S.

Amends

How many pages?
  How long would my list have to be?

There was a lot of harm.
  I was ready to make amends for it all.

Adam L.S.

Just Do It

A new kind of honesty…

Forgive others, and maybe I am forgiven.
I cut away my justifications.

Adam L.S.

It's Possible

These barriers seemed impossible,
  but they were not.

I would not be blocked,
  by fear or pride.

So I made amends,
  wherever possible.

Adam L.S.

Best Of The Best

I had to accept things,
  my decisions,
  my actions and their reactions.

I had to do this to the best of my ability.

Adam L.S.

Almost There

Was this beyond my means?
  I did not want to fail.

I'd reach out.
  I'd take guidance.

Adam L.S.

Unresolved

It was unresolved however…
  I'd do my part.
  I'd consider my past wrongs.
  I'd make my amends.
  I'd let go of bitterness.

I was filled with joy.

Adam L.S.

Wrong

I was wrong…

I could not wait around,
  I could not take time to "figure it out."

So I promptly admitted it.

Adam L.S.

Searching

I'm always searching for ways to avoid them,
  wreckage and pain.

Not just from my past,
  but from in my present.

Adam L.S.

Difficulties

I was so hungry,
  angry…
  lonely…
  tired…

That was my old pattern,
  that was the old insanity,
  that was me suffering,
  that felt like a hole in the gut.

Adam L.S.

Counter Clockwise

Like a pleasure relief valve spun,
 no more rationalizing,
 no more running,
 no more fighting.

All it took was a simple twist,
 I was amazed.

Adam L.S.

Examine

This is a privilege,
  this life,
  this feeling,
  this world.

It is like a fantasy,
  just being here,
  it feels good.

Adam L.S.

Higher Power

This conversation will continue,
  I will do whatever it takes to remain in contact.

You have so much knowledge,
  You have have so much power.

Adam L.S.

Your Will

I understand now,
  this foundation is so beautiful.

The steps do not end,
  the growth does not end.

I will continue praying,
  I will continue working,
  I will continue improving.

Adam L.S.

Clock Struck

This message,
  is your message,
  I will carry it,
  wherever I go.

These principles,
  are your principles,
  I will practice them,
  in all my affairs.

Adam L.S.

More Meaning

I never expected all of this,
this spiritual awakening.

I just wanted to stop hurting,
now I can truly live.

Adam L.S.

Also by Adam L.S.

The Tradition is poetry exploring our welfare, our purpose, our spiritual foundation. How carrying a message to anyone who is suffering is a beautiful tradition.

The Tradition
Coming soon!

www.ingramcontent.com/pod-product-compliance
Lightning Source LLC
LaVergne TN
LVHW050317160826
845677LV00014B/3443

* 9 7 9 8 2 2 7 9 2 2 6 9 4 *